SHIMMER & Shine™

Sticker Activity Book

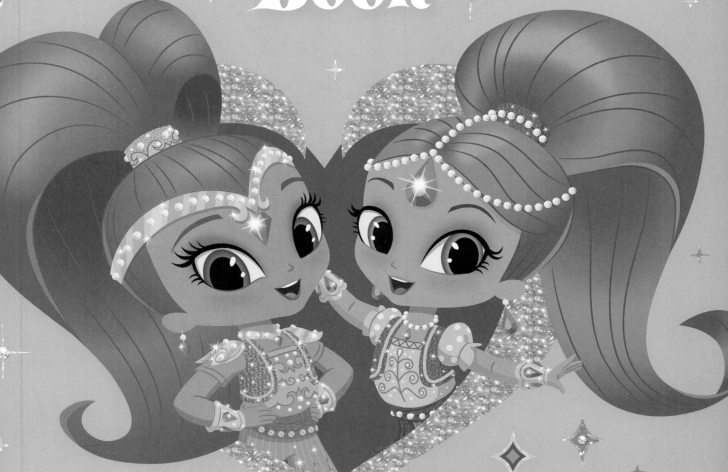

D1332955

centum

Meet the genies

Add some colour to this picture of the magical sisters, Shimmer and Shine, on their flying carpet.

Stick a Tala sticker here.

Shimmer is a sweet, loveable ball of energy. She loves to have fun with her sister, Shine, and her pet monkey, Tala.

Stick a Nahal sticker here.

Shine is bold, kind and lots of fun.
She is a caring sister to her genie twin,
Shimmer, and adores her pet tiger, Nahal.

Magical pets

Help Tala and Nahal count up all the objects in the groups below.

A

B

C

Shimmer's cheeky pet monkey, Tala, loves dressing up and shiny objects.

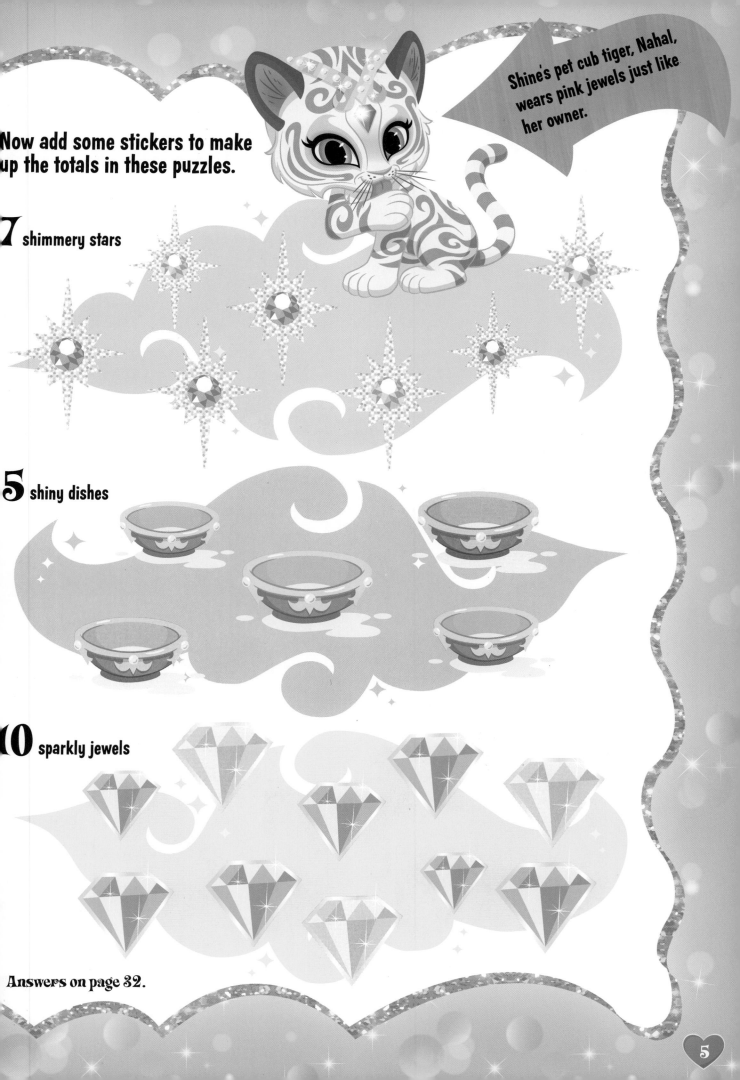

Now add some stickers to make up the totals in these puzzles.

Shine's pet cub tiger, Nahal, wears pink jewels just like her owner.

7 shimmery stars

5 shiny dishes

10 sparkly jewels

Answers on page 32.

Double trouble

Can you spot 7 differences between these pictures of Shimmer and Shine?

Too easy? Now try and find 10 differences between these pictures too.

Answers on page 32.

Magical maze

Help Shimmer and Shine fly their magic carpet through the cloud maze to reach their home in Zahramay Falls.

Start

Finish

How many rainbows did you spot along the way?

Answers on page 32.

Perfect path

Which path should Shimmer take to reach her sister Shine in The Garden of the Hanging Stars?

A

B

C

D

E

Which paths take Shimmer right back to where she started?

Answers on page 32.

Dazzling pairs

Shimmer and Shine have mixed up all their sparkly
gems and jewels. Can you help them match them into pairs?

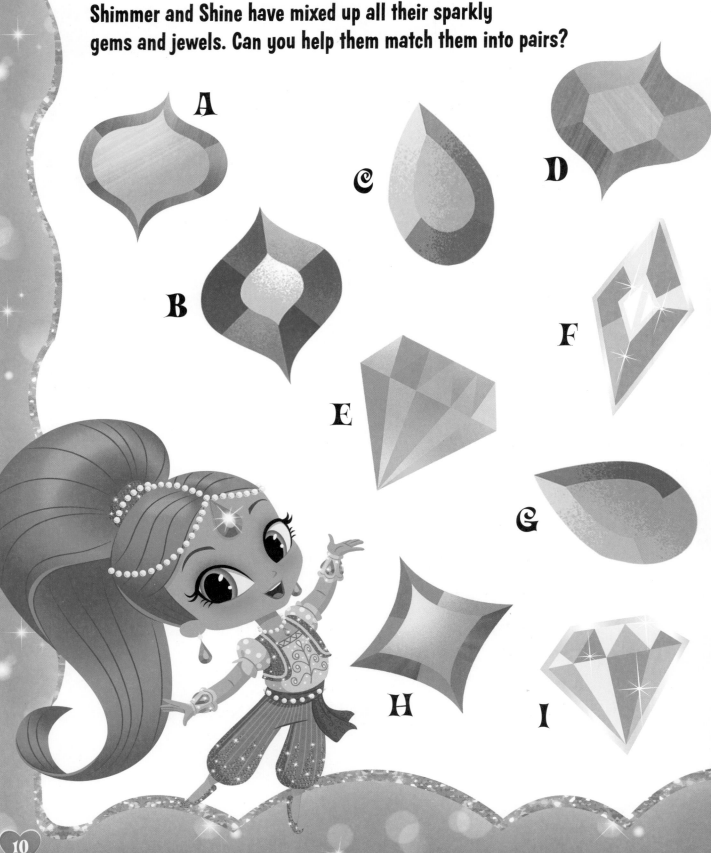

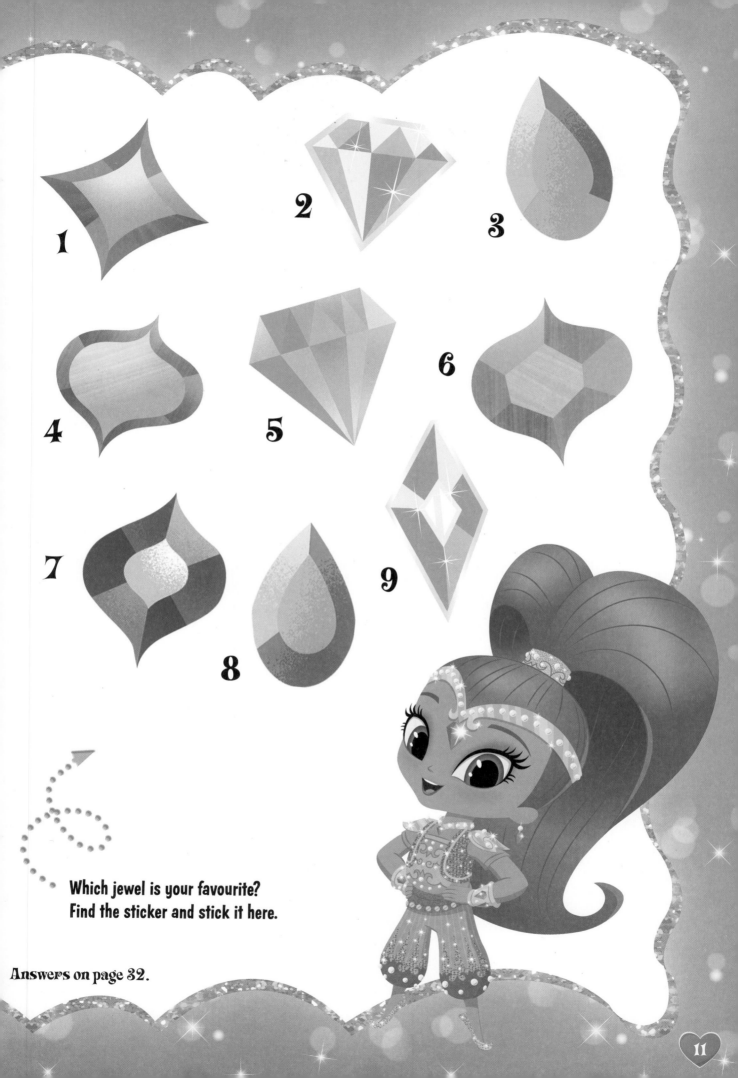

1

2

3

4

5

6

7

8

9

Which jewel is your favourite?
Find the sticker and stick it here.

Answers on page 32.

11

Oopsie!

Leah is wishing for all the things she loves, but the genie sisters keep making mistakes. Can you spot the odd one out in each row?

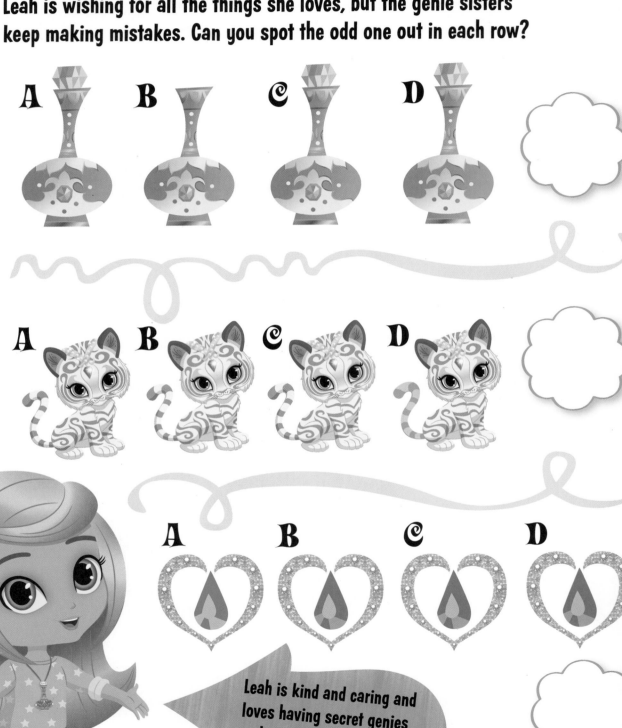

Leah is kind and caring and loves having secret genies as her best friends.

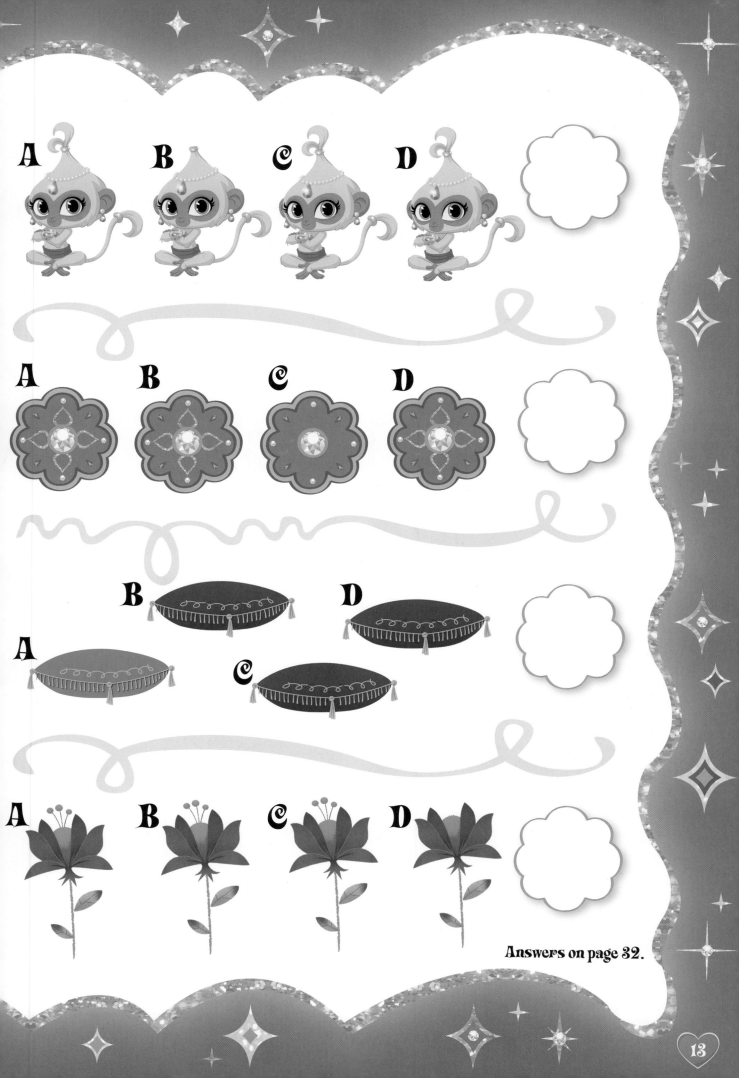

A **B** **C** **D**

A **B** **C** **D**

B **D** **A** **C**

A **B** **C** **D**

Answers on page 32.

13

Make a wish!

Join the dots to reveal what Leah is wishing for and help the genie sisters make her wish come true.

Don't forget to colour it in.

Oh my genie!

These smaller pictures may look the same as the big picture but they're not. Can you spot what's different in each one?

A

B

C

Shimmer and Shine often make mistakes as genies-in-training but their mistakes turn out great when they work together.

Answers on page 32.

Wishing game

Help Shimmer and Shine make Leah's wish, to ride on a magic carpet, come true with this fun game. You can play it with a friend or on your own.

Start

1. Hop on the magic carpet and fly on 3 clouds.

2.

3.

4. Name Leah's best friend and have another go.

5.

6.

7. Oopsie! You forgot Nahal and Tala, go back to the start.

8. Stop to practise some wishes and miss a go.

9.

1. Stick your Shimmer and Shine player stickers on a coin.
2. Take it turns to roll the dice and move across the board.
3. Follow the instructions when you land on each cloud.
4. The first player across the board helps make Leah's wish come true and wins the game.

16. A helpful genie tells you a shortcut, go ahead 3 clouds.

14.

15.

13.

17.

18. Tala and Nahal need a nap, go back to the start.

12. Stop for an ice cream and miss a go.

19. You find a lucky jewel. Have another go.

11.

10. Oopsie! You bump into a star. Go back 2 clouds.

20.

Finish

Divine jumble

Can you find the right stickers to complete this picture of Leah and her friend Zac?

Now add some stickers to finish this picture of Nahal and Tala too.

Like her owner, Shine, Nahal is brave and feisty, but can also be a bit of a scaredy-cat too.

Answers on page 32.

19

Be jeweled

Take a look at the pretty patterns below then find the sticker to complete the sequences.

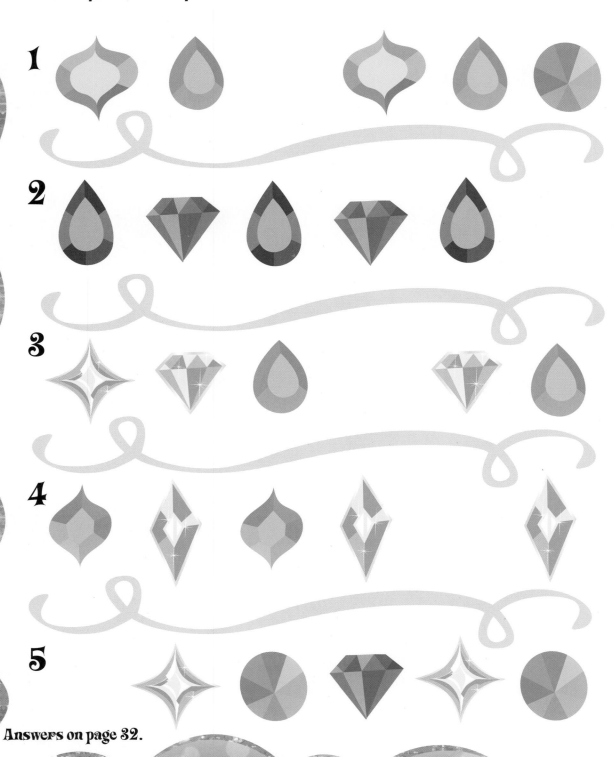

1

2

3

4

5

Answers on page 32.

Sparkle spot

Help Leah and Zac work out the difference between big and small in the puzzles below.

Draw a circle around the smallest jewel.

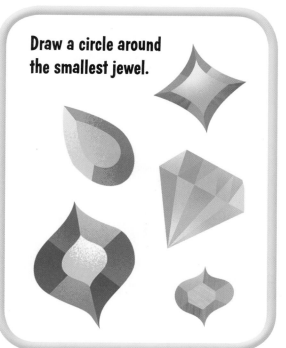

Colour in the biggest genie bottle.

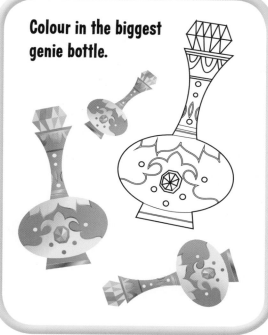

Put a tick next to the biggest flower.

Can you find a sticker of a bigger star than these ones?

Answers on page 32.

Lots to spot

Shimmer and Shine are playing hide and seek.
Can you help them find all the things in the picture below?

Put a tick next to them when you spot them.

Answers on page 32.

Genie Fun

Help Shimmer and Shine out of their genie bottle by finding the stars and tracing over the letters inside to reveal the sisters' secret power.

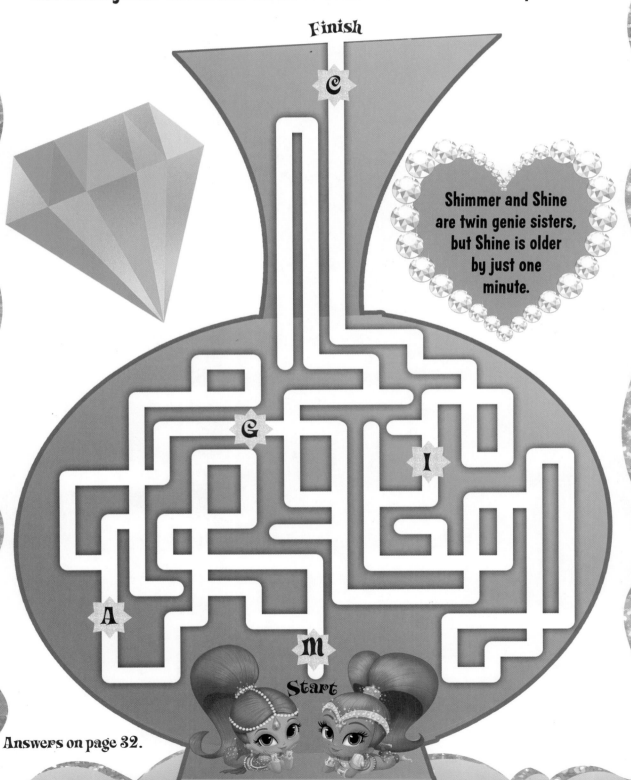

Finish

Shimmer and Shine are twin genie sisters, but Shine is older by just one minute.

Start

Answers on page 32.

24

Glitter friends

Add a splash of colour to this picture of Shimmer and Shine in their genie outfits.

Don't forget to add some jewel stickers to give them extra sparkle.

Picture perfect

Oopsie! Tala has spilt ice cream on Shimmer's favourite picture. Can you work out which of the pictures below are the covered parts?

Tala's curious nature often leads her into mischief.

1

2

3

4

5

Answers on page 32.

Shadow spot

Leah has wished for a midnight feast and is playing a shadow game with her genie friends. Which shadow belongs to who?

A

B

C

D

E

1

2

3

4

5

Answers on page 32.

Oodles of doodles

Grab your pens and crayons to finish off these doodles and drawings.

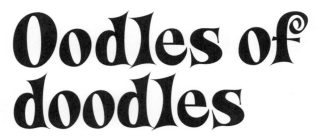

Add some colour to this picture of Leah.

Doodle some hair onto Shimmer and Shine.

Join the dots to help the genie sisters fly.

5 4 3 2 1   20 19 18
6   16 17
7   15
8 9 10 11   13 14
         12

What would you wish for if Shimmer and Shine were your genies? Draw it here.

Sweet and sparkly

Create a fun picture with your stickers.
Don't forget to add lots of glitter
and stars for extra sparkles!

Answers

Check your answers to all the fun puzzles, games and activities here.

Page 4   A, 6 B, 7 C, 5

Page 5

Page 6

Page 7

Page 8

12 rainbows

Page 9 C, paths B and D lead back to Shimmer

Page 10-11 A, 4 B, 7 C, 8 D, 6 E, 5 F, 9 G, 3 H, 1 I, 2

Page 12-13 B, D, A, B, C, A, D

Page 15

A   B   C

Page 18

Page 19

Page 20

1.   2.   3.   4.   5.

Page 21

Page 22-23

Page 24

magic

Page 26 A, 4 B, 3 C, 2 D, 5 E, 1

Page 27 A, 3 B ,4 C, 2 D, 5 E, 1

P2-3

P11

P5

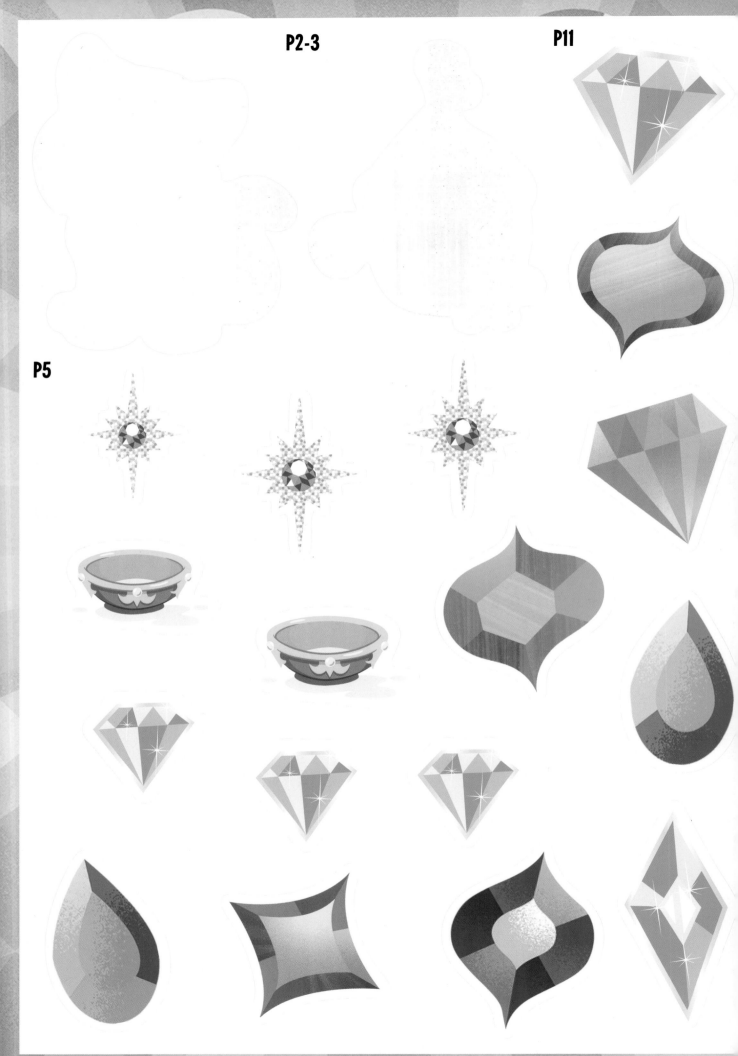

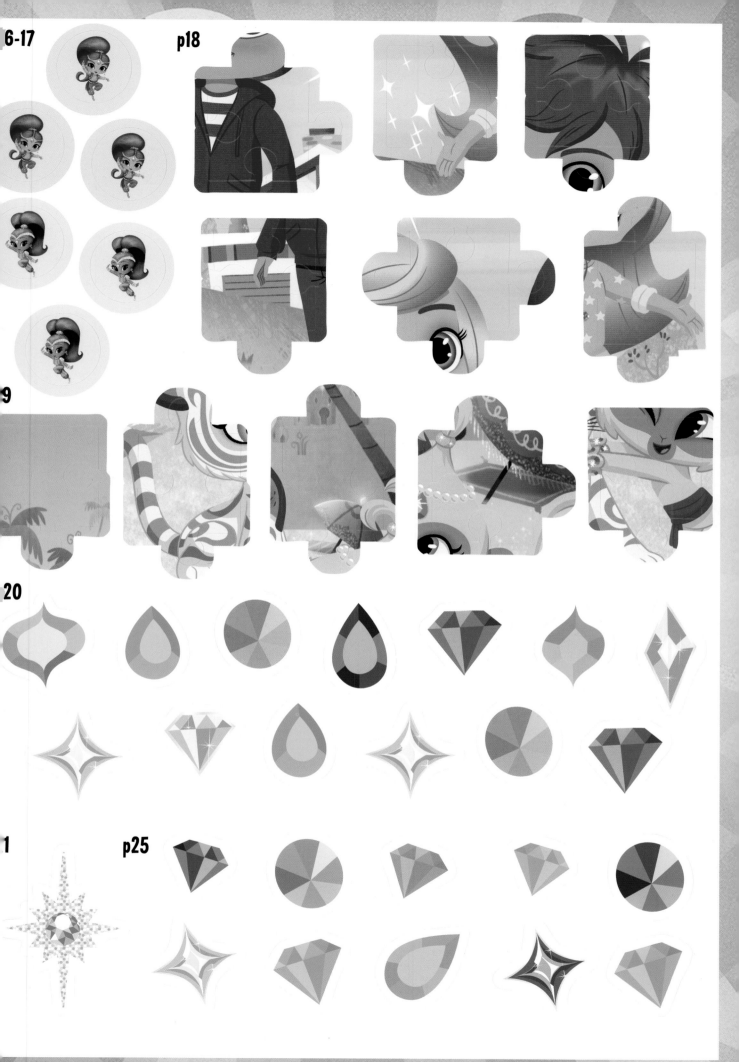

p6-17

p18

p19

p20

p21 p25

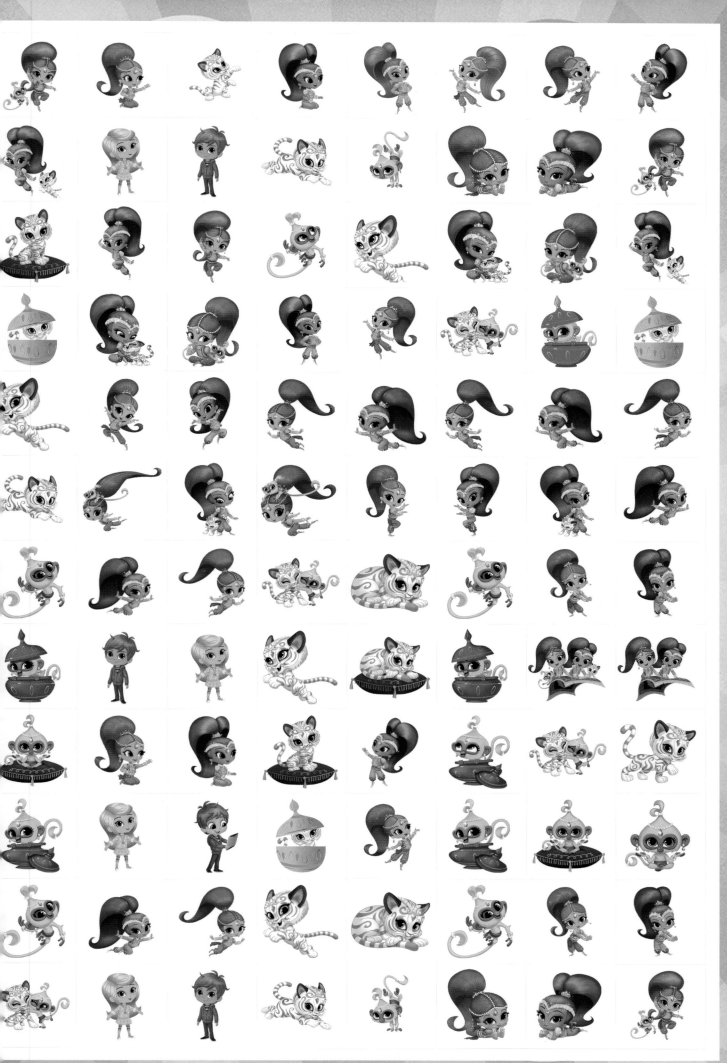

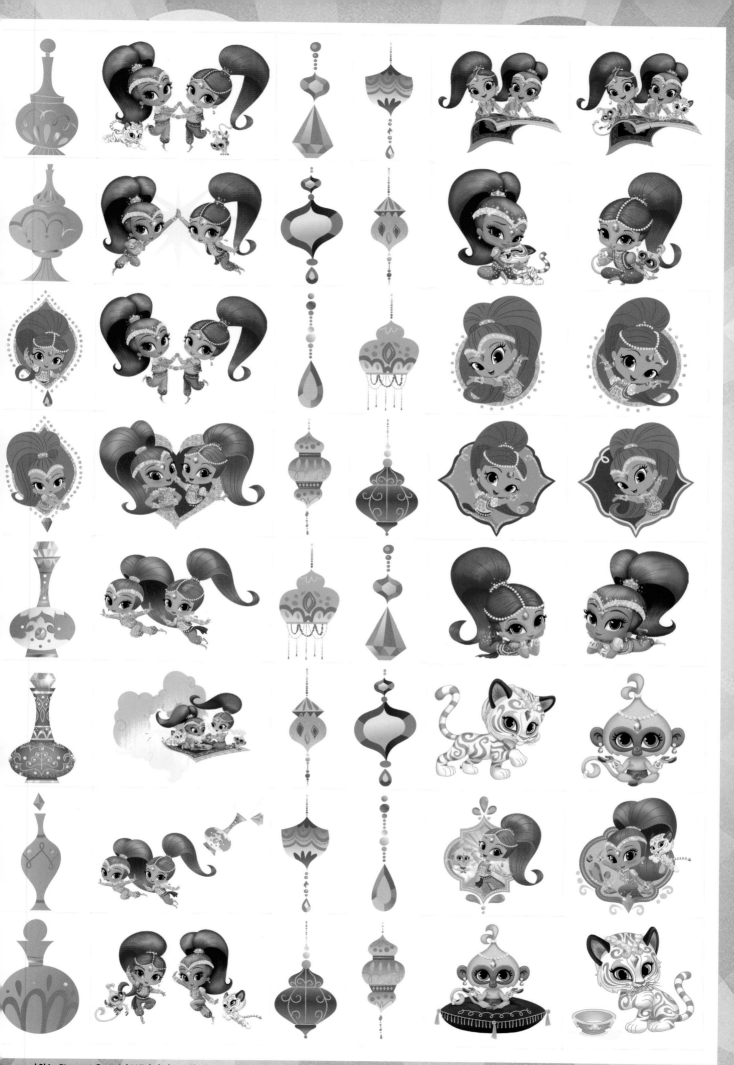

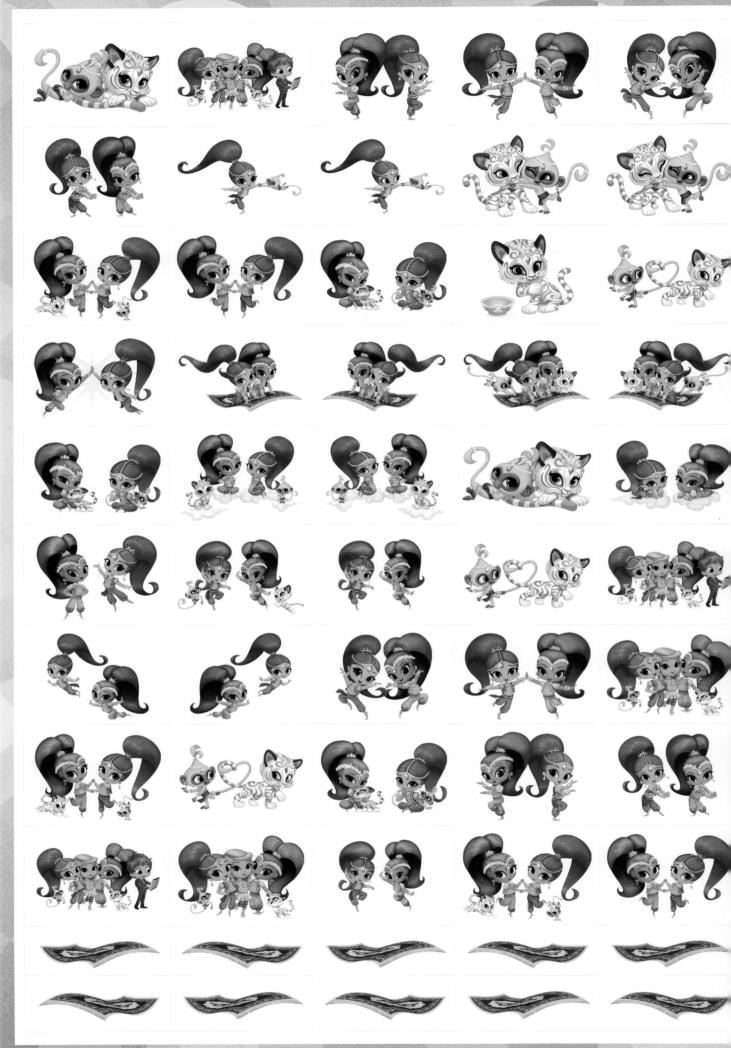